NEW YORK REVIEW BOOKS

POETS

JACK SPICER (1925–1965) was a poet and linguist born in Los Angeles, California. At the University of California, Berkeley, he became close friends with the poets Robin Blaser and Robert Duncan, and with them he went on to play a central role in the San Francisco Renaissance of the late 1940s and the 1950s. During his life, Spicer published six short books of poetry, all with small, local presses. He died of alcohol poisoning in the poverty ward of San Francisco General Hospital. Posthumous editions of his work include *My Vocabulary Did This to Me: The Collected Poetry of Jack Spicer*, *The House That Jack Built: The Collected Lectures of Jack Spicer*, and *Be Brave to Things: The Uncollected Poetry and Plays of Jack Spicer*.

PETER GIZZI is the author of many collections of poetry, most recently *Now It's Dark* and *Archeophonics* (a finalist for the 2016 National Book Award). His honors include fellowships from the Rex Foundation, the Howard Foundation, the Foundation for Contemporary Arts, and the John Simon Guggenheim Memorial Foundation. His editing projects have included *The House That Jack Built: The Collected Lectures of Jack Spicer* and, with Kevin Killian, *My Vocabulary Did This to Me: The Collected Poetry of Jack Spicer*. He works at the University of Massachusetts, Amherst.

T0046959

Jack Spicer

After Lorca

PREFACE BY PETER GIZZI

NYRB/POETS

 NEW YORK REVIEW BOOKS   *New York*

THIS IS A NEW YORK REVIEW BOOK
PUBLISHED BY THE NEW YORK REVIEW OF BOOKS
435 Hudson Street, New York, NY 10014
www.nyrb.com

First published by New York Review Books in 2021.

Library of Congress Cataloging-in-Publication Data
Names: Spicer, Jack, author. | Gizzi, Peter, writer of preface.
Title: After Lorca / by Jack Spicer; preface by Peter Gizzi.
Description: New York City: New York Review Books, [2021] |
   Series: New York Review Books poets
Identifiers: LCCN 2020013632 (print) | LCCN 2020013633 (ebook) |
   ISBN 9781681375410 (paperback) | ISBN 9781681375427 (ebook)
Subjects: LCGFT: Poetry.
Classification: LCC PS3569.P47 A7 2021 (print) | LCC PS3569.P47 (ebook) |
   DDC 811/.54—dc23
LC record available at https://lccn.loc.gov/2020013632
LC ebook record available at https://lccn.loc.gov/2020013633

ISBN 978-1-68137-541-0
Available as an electronic book; ISBN 978-1-68137-542-7

Cover and book design by Emily Singer

Printed in the United States of America on acid-free paper.
10 9 8 7 6 5 4 3 2 1

This edition of **After Lorca** *is dedicated to Kevin Killian*

Contents

WHEN JACK SPICER DIED in 1965 of alcoholism in the poverty ward of the San Francisco General Hospital at the age of forty, his last words were, "My vocabulary did this to me." These are hard words, words spoken by a man who was not only a trained linguist but also a queer, brilliant, ruthlessly honest poet of heartbreak who wrote that "loneliness is necessary for pure poetry."

What can be said about Spicer? Was he a genius? Certainly. Was he difficult? Undoubtedly. Was he fiercely true to his art? Absolutely. Did he push back against the commercialization of bohemia? Yes, and throughout his life he eschewed copyright. He published his work with small local presses in editions of no more than five hundred copies, and even went so far as to restrict their distribution to the Bay Area. Still, over the last sixty years his work has gained a wide and devoted international readership. This legacy and the mastery that ensured it began with *After Lorca*, Spicer's first book, in which he boldly and gleefully transforms modernism into a séance.

Spicer was born in 1925 in Southern California, although he claimed his birth year to be 1946, the year he met the poets Robert Duncan and Robin Blaser at the University of California, Berkeley, where they studied with the German medievalist Ernst Kantorowicz and the poet Josephine Miles. Out of the intense fraternity of these three gay, bookish young men the San Francisco Renaissance was born. While Spicer spent the majority of his adult life in the Bay Area, a yearlong excursion to New York and Boston in 1955 defined the development of his poetic vision, even as his time on the East Coast solidified his allegiance to the American West and his identity as a California poet. When he returned to San Francisco, he taught his now famous Poetry As Magic workshop and was employed as a researcher in linguistics at UC Berkeley. In 1965, shortly before his death, he gave four important lectures on his poetry and poetics.

Spicer was an erudite poet, with a knowledge of Latin, German, Spanish, French, Old Norse, and Old English; he is also one of our great poets of love and abjection. Foul-mouthed and cranky, certainly alcoholic, Spicer was a devotional poet who wrote at the intersection of doubt, irreverence, and belief. At his favorite local bar, he organized and presided over Blabbermouth Night, an event at which poets were encouraged to babble, to speak in tongues. Linguistic sound mattered to him. As a researcher at UC Berkeley, he worked for years mapping slight changes in vowel sounds from town to town in Northern California, a project that is reflected in his later books *Language* and *Book of Magazine Verse*.

In the context of his time Spicer was bohemian rather than Beat. In the late 1940s, he hosted the maverick folklorist Harry Smith on the first radio show devoted to folk music at KPFA. He also subverted the earnestness of the folk movement by presenting his own songs on the air as chanteys his friends had just collected down on the pier. He delighted in provocative and incongruous combinations, and from the beginning he was both fascinated with and troubled by notions of authenticity, likening the search for origins to a grail quest. He would later interrogate such endeavors in his book *The Holy Grail*:

I have forgotten why the grail was important
Why somebody wants to reach it like a window you
    throw open. Thrown open
What could it mean?

In all this, he was working toward a renewed and expanded sense of literary tradition, one that is closer to the dynamic transmission common in folk cultures than to the hierarchies of "who begat whom" prized by the English departments of the period. Folk transmission is a useful way to understand Spicer's attraction to Federico García Lorca, given Lorca's long-standing interest in and study of Gypsy ballads.

As for *After Lorca*, its roots lie not in California but in Boston. During his year there, Spicer worked at the Boston Public Library in Copley Square and occasionally wrote reviews for *The Boston Public Library Quarterly*. Reviewing the three-volume edition of *The Complete Poems of Emily Dickinson* edited by Thomas Johnson, Spicer makes a prescient and original reading emphasizing the close commerce between Dickinson's poetry and her prose:

The reason for the difficulty of drawing a line between the poetry and prose in Emily Dickinson's letters may be that she did not wish such a line to be drawn. If large portions of her correspondence are considered not as mere letters—and, indeed, they seldom communicate information, or have much to do with the person to whom they were written—but as experiments in a heightened prose combined with poetry, a new approach to both her letters and her poetry opens up.

A year later, back in San Francisco, Spicer would explore this porous boundary further in his own books of poems *After Lorca* and *Admonitions* (published posthumously). Here he developed his notion of "correspondence," making letters essential to the structure of the book; the approach draws on his reading of Dickinson, and possibly echoes Baudelaire, but also displays a characteristic humor, in that Spicer literally incorporates letters in his books. For Spicer, correspondence takes on the aura of a conversation between spirits, a kind of voicing that lives beyond the grave. "That is how we dead men write to each other," he says. Reading through *After Lorca*, it becomes clear that Spicer's radical reconfiguring of the concept of correspondence was central for his work on many levels through letters, translation, and his redefinition of tradition. We discover that "things do not connect; they correspond."

After Lorca was published by White Rabbit Press in 1957. Spicer was thirty-two and had been writing poetry seriously for a decade. But he turned his back on all that work, much of it brilliant, and considered *After Lorca* to be the beginning of his "real work." With it he establishes not only his distinctive idea of correspondence but also a new concept of composition by book—the book not as a collection but as a community of poems that "echo and re-echo against each other" to "create resonances." As Spicer has it: "Poems cannot live alone any more than we can."

After Lorca exemplifies Spicer's macabre humor, serious gamesmanship, and unfettered troubling of the notions of originality and authenticity in poetic composition, which begs the question of who is speaking in a poem. The book's introduction can be read as a Dadaist send-up of the venerable Yale Series of Younger Poets. In the 1950s, W. H. Auden was its judge, championing books by Rosalie Moore, Adrienne Rich, W. S. Merwin, John Ashbery, and James Wright. Adapting the convention of an established older poet vetting and presenting the emerging poet, Spicer brings back the martyred Lorca from the grave to speak on the living poet's behalf. Understandably put out, Lorca begins: "Frankly I was quite surprised when Mr. Spicer asked me to write an introduction to this volume." Spicer's provocative poetics of engaging the dead in his literary practice begins with a joke, albeit deadpan.

Lorca of course is unlikely to help the poet get reviewed, find an agent, place a second book, or secure a job. As a reluctant interlocutor who happens to be long dead, Lorca doesn't possess any cultural capital that could be helpful to Spicer. But his position offers more to an orphic poet like Spicer than would a conventional blessing from any established figure: a singular, live connection to the underworld, a perfect vehicle for the subject of unrequited love, and an ideal emblem of the unconventional notions of literary inheritance and tradition the younger poet values.

After Lorca is ostensibly composed of translations of

Lorca's work, the faithfulness of which Lorca questions. There are also eleven original Spicer poems masquerading as translations, combined with six "programmatic" letters to Lorca in which Spicer articulates his poetics and his personal woes about poetry, love, and his contemporaries.* With these letters, creative translations, and fake translations, Spicer places himself in opposition to both Romantic and confessional poetics by disavowing the notion of the poet as a "beautiful machine...almost a perpetual motion machine of emotion until the poet's heart broke or it was burned on the beach like Shelley's." Spicer insists on the fact that the poet does not drive the poem; the poem drives the poet. Instead of becoming a master of words, the poet is mastered by words, which "turn mysteriously against those who use them."

Throughout *After Lorca*, Spicer marries poetry and poetics with an electric sense of innovation. And he found a way to have his cake and eat it too. You'd think the presence of ars poetica would make it *easier* to discuss the work or would tend to define and delimit the poem, but in Spicer it only complicates things, making its meaning no easier to decipher. The hybrid of poem and poetics can't be instrumentalized. It is a mode that he would continue to develop and extend in his later work through a resonant practice of deep listening, which he would call "dictation." Spicer reminds us that

---

*The "original" Spicer poems masquerading as Lorca translations are "Ballad of the Seven Passages," "Frog," "A Diamond," "The Ballad of the Dead Woodcutter," "Alba," "Aquatic Park," "Ballad of Sleeping Somewhere Else," "Buster Keaton Rides Again: A Sequel," "Friday, the 13th," "Afternoon," and "Radar."

poetry is an ancient medium meant to return the dead to the world of light and speech. He would write later that "The ghosts the poems were written for are the ghosts of the poems. We have it second-hand. They cannot hear the noise they have been making." He's covering Lorca, not quite in the way a rock band covers a tune but in the way a bandage covers a fatal wound. Poetry cuts deep. Lorca may have been murdered, but he's alive in this book and now too is Spicer. At its root, poetry is a haunted practice, calling to the dead, crossing boundaries again and again. Its power can seize the invisible and give it purchase in our world.

The first letter to Lorca describes tradition as "generations of different poets in different countries patiently telling the same story, writing the same poem." Here Spicer takes his place among poets who comprise a class of workers, all of them engaged in the same basic project. Despite *After Lorca*'s frames and baffles, or perhaps because of them, Spicer's first book offers us a pure lyric poetry, with all its attendant concerns: divinity and accident, physical beauty and romantic love, political outrage and enlightenment. These frames only renew the power of the lyric to stun us, awaken us to a new reality. A lyric reality.

—*Peter Gizzi*

After Lorca

With an Introduction by Federico García Lorca

(1957)

INTRODUCTION

FRANKLY I WAS QUITE SURPRISED when Mr. Spicer asked me to write an introduction to this volume. My reaction to the manuscript he sent me (and to the series of letters that are now a part of it) was and is fundamentally unsympathetic. It seems to me the waste of a considerable talent on something which is not worth doing. However, I have been removed from all contact with poetry for the last twenty years. The younger generation of poets may view with pleasure Mr. Spicer's execution of what seems to me a difficult and unrewarding task.

It must be made clear at the start that these poems are not translations. In even the most literal of them Mr. Spicer seems to derive pleasure in inserting or substituting one or two words which completely change the mood and often the meaning of the poem as I had written it. More often he takes one of my poems and adjoins to half of it another half of his own, giving rather the effect of an unwilling centaur. (Modesty forbids me to speculate which end of the animal is mine.)

Finally there are an almost equal number of poems that I did not write at all (one supposes they must be his) executed in a somewhat fanciful imitation of my earlier style. The reader is given no indication which of the poems belong to which category, and I have further complicated the problem (with malice aforethought I must admit) by sending Mr. Spicer several poems written after my death which he has also translated and included here. Even the most faithful student of my work will be hard put to decide what is and what is not García Lorca as, indeed, he would if he were to look into my present resting place. The analogy is impolite, but I fear the impoliteness is deserved.

The letters are another problem. When Mr. Spicer began sending them to me a few months ago, I recognized immediately the "programmatic letter"—the letter one poet writes to another not in any effort to communicate with him, but rather as a young man whispers his secrets to a scarecrow, knowing that his young lady is in the distance listening. The young lady in this case may be a Muse, but the scarecrow nevertheless quite naturally resents the confidences. The reader, who is not a party to this singular tryst, may be amused by what he overhears.

The dead are notoriously hard to satisfy. Mr. Spicer's mixture may please his contemporary audience or may, and this is more probable, lead him to write better poetry of his own. But I am strongly reminded as I survey this curious amalgam of a cartoon published in an American magazine while I was visiting your country in New York. The cartoon showed a gravestone on which were inscribed the words: "HERE LIES AN OFFICER AND A GENTLEMAN." The caption below it read: "I wonder how they happened to be buried in the same grave?"

Federico García Lorca
Outside Granada, October 1957

Juan Ramón Jiménez

A Translation for John Ryan

In the white endlessness
Snow, seaweed, and salt
He lost his imagination.

The color white. He walks
Upon a soundless carpet made
Of pigeon feathers.

Without eyes or thumbs
He suffers a dream not moving
But the bones quiver.

In the white endlessness
How pure and big a wound
His imagination left.

Snow, seaweed, and salt. Now
In the white endlessness.

Ballad of the Little Girl Who Invented the Universe

A Translation for George Stanley

Jasmine flower and a bull with his throat slashed.
Infinite sidewalk. Map. Room. Harp. Sunrise.
A little girl pretends a bull made of jasmine
And the bull is a bloody twilight that bellows.

If the sky could be a little boy
The jasmines could take half the night to themselves
And the bull a blue bullring of his own
With his heart at the foot of a small column.

But the sky is an elephant
And the jasmines are water without blood
And the little girl is a bouquet of night flowers
Lost on a big dark sidewalk.

Between the jasmine and the bull
Or the hooks of the sleeping people of marble or
In the jasmine, clouds and an elephant—
The skeleton of a little girl turning.

Dear Lorca,

These letters are to be as temporary as our poetry is to be permanent. They will establish the bulk, the wastage that my sour-stomached contemporaries demand to help them swallow and digest the pure word. We will use up our rhetoric here so that it will not appear in our poems. Let it be consumed paragraph by paragraph, day by day, until nothing of it is left in our poetry and nothing of our poetry is left in it. It is precisely because these letters are unnecessary that they must be written.

In my last letter I spoke of the tradition. The fools that read these letters will think by this we mean what tradition seems to have meant lately—an historical patchwork (whether made up of Elizabethan quotations, guide books of the poet's home town, or obscure bits of magic published by Pantheon) which is used to cover up the nakedness of the bare word. Tradition means much more than that. It means generations of different poets in different countries patiently telling the same story, writing the same poem, gaining and losing something with each transformation—but, of course, never really losing anything. This has nothing to do with calmness, classicism, temperament, or anything else. Invention is merely the enemy of poetry.

See how weak prose is. I invent a word like invention. These paragraphs could be translated, transformed by a chain of fifty poets in fifty languages, and they still would be temporary, untrue, unable to yield the substance of a single image. Prose invents—poetry discloses.

A mad man is talking to himself in the room next to mine. He speaks in prose. Presently I shall go to a bar and there one or two poets will speak to me and I to them and we will try to destroy each other or attract each other or even listen to each other and nothing will happen because we will be speaking in prose. I will go home, drunken and dissatisfied, and sleep—and my dreams will be prose. Even the sub-conscious is not patient enough for poetry.

You are dead and the dead are very patient.

Love,
Jack

Ballad of the Seven Passages

A Translation for Ebbe Borregaard

Rimbaud is spelled with seven letters of the alphabet
Your heart will never break at what you are hearing
Rimbaud was older than you are when he was dead
Your heart will never break at what you are hearing.
I tell you, darling, beauty was never as old as he was
And your heart will never break at what you are hearing.
Shut your mouth.
Rimbaud is spelled with seven passages
A E I O U Y
And that stony vowel called death.
Oh,
Damn Rimbaud,
Beauty is spelled with all the vowels of seven passages.
Shut your damned mouth.
When Rimbaud died he became older than your alphabet
And your heart will never break at what you are hearing.

Debussy

A Translation for the University of Redlands

My shadow moves silently
Upon the water in the ditch.

Upon my shadow are the frogs
Blocked off from the stars.

The shadow demands from my body
Unmoving images.

My shadow skims the water like a huge
Violet-colored mosquito.

A hundred crickets try to mine gold
From the light in the rushes.

A light born in my heart
Upon the ditch, reflected.

Frog

A Translation for Graham Mackintosh

Like all the novels I've read
My mind is going to a climax
And a climax means a splash in the pool.
Bóoing. Bóoing. Bóoing.
And your heart is full of water
And your nose can't hardly breathe.
Remember
How black those pinetrees were that fire burned.
All that black forest. And the noise
(Splash)
Of a single green needle.

Buster Keaton's Ride

A Translation for Melvin Bakkerud

ROOSTER: Cockledoodledoo!

(Buster Keaton enters carrying four children in his arms.)

BUSTER KEATON (takes out a wooden dagger and kills them): My poor children!

ROOSTER: Cockledoodledoo!

BUSTER KEATON (counting the corpses on the ground): One, two, three, four. (Grabs a bicycle and goes.)

(Among the old rubber tires and cans of gasoline a Negro eats a straw hat.)

BUSTER KEATON: What a beautiful afternoon!

(A parrot flutters around in the sexless sky.)

BUSTER KEATON: I like riding a bicycle.

THE OWL: Toowit toowoo.

BUSTER KEATON: How beautifully these birds sing!

THE OWL: Hoo!

BUSTER KEATON: It's lovely!

(Pause. Buster Keaton ineffably crosses the rushes and little fields of rye. The landscape shortens itself beneath the wheels of his machine. The bicycle has a single dimension. It is able to enter books and to expand itself even into operas and coalmines. The bicycle of Buster Keaton does not have a riding seat of caramel or sugar pedals like the bicycles bad men ride. It is a bicycle like all bicycles except for a unique drenching of innocence. Adam and Eve run by, frightened as if they were carrying a vase full of water and, in passing, pet the bicycle of Buster Keaton.)

BUSTER KEATON: Ah, love, love!

(Buster Keaton falls to the ground. The bicycle escapes him. It runs behind two enormous gray butterflies. It skims madly half an inch from the ground.)

BUSTER KEATON: I don't want to talk. Won't somebody please say something?

A VOICE: Fool!

(He continues walking. His eyes, infinite and sad like a newly born animal, dream of lilies and angels and silken belts. His eyes which are like the bottom of a vase. His eyes of a mad child. Which are most faithful. Which are most beautiful. The eyes of an ostrich. His human eyes with a secure equipoise with melancholy. Philadelphia is seen in the distance. The inhabitants of that city now know that the old poem of a Singer machine is able to encircle the big roses of the green-house but not at all to comprehend the poetic difference between a bowl of hot tea and a bowl of cold tea. Philadelphia shines in the distance.)

(An American girl with eyes of celluloid comes through the grass.)

BUSTER KEATON: Hello.

(Buster Keaton smiles and looks at the shoes of the girl. Those shoes! We do not have to admire her shoes. It would take a crocodile to wear them.)

BUSTER KEATON: I would have liked—

THE AMERICAN (breathless): Do you carry a sword decked with myrtle leaves?

(Buster Keaton shrugs his shoulders and lifts his right foot.)

THE AMERICAN: Do you have a ring with a poisoned stone?

(Buster Keaton twists slowly and lifts an inquiring leg.)

THE AMERICAN: Well?

(Four angels with wings of a heavenly gas balloon piss among the flowers. The ladies of the town play a piano as if they were riding a bicycle. The waltz, a moon, and seventeen Indian canoes rock the precious heart of our friend. As the greatest surprise of all, autumn has invaded the garden like water explodes a geometrical clump of sugar.)

BUSTER KEATON (sighing): I would have liked to have been a swan. But I can't do what I would have liked.

Because—What happened to my hat? Where is my collar of little birds and my mohair necktie? What a disgrace!

(A young girl with a wasp waist and a high collar comes in on a bicycle. She has the head of a nightingale.)

YOUNG GIRL: Whom do I have the honor of saluting?

BUSTER KEATON (with a bow): Buster Keaton.

(The young girl faints and falls off the bicycle. Her legs on the ground tremble like two agonized cobras. A gramophone plays a thousand versions of the same song—"In Philadelphia they have no nightingales.")

BUSTER KEATON (kneeling): Darling Miss Eleanor, pardon me! (lower) Darling (lower still) Darling (lowest) Darling.

(The lights of Philadelphia flicker and go out in the faces of a thousand policemen.)

Ballad of the Shadowy Pigeons

A Translation for Joe Dunn

On the branches of laurel
Saw two shadowy pigeons.
One of them was the sun
The other the moon.

Little neighbors, I asked them,
Where am I buried?
In my tail, said the sun.
In my craw, said the moon.

And I who had been walking
With the earth at my waistline
Saw two eagles of marble
And a naked maiden.
The one was the other
And the maiden was no one.

Little eagles, I asked them,
Where am I buried?
In my tail, said the sun.
In my craw, said the moon.

On the branches of laurel
Saw two naked pigeons.
The one was the other
And the both of them no one.

Suicide

A Translation for Eric Weir

At ten o'clock in the morning
The young man could not remember.

His heart was stuffed with dead wings
And linen flowers.

He is conscious that there is nothing left
In his mouth but one word.

When he removes his coat soft ashes
Fall from his arms.

Through the window he sees a tower
He sees a window and a tower.

His watch has run down in its case
He observes the way it was looking at him.

He sees his shadow stretched
Upon a white silk cushion.

And the stiff geometric youngster
Shatters the mirror with an ax.

The mirror submerges everything
In a great spurt of shadow.

Bacchus

A Translation for Don Allen

An untouched green murmur.
The figtree wants to extend me its branches.

Like a panther its shadow
Stalks my poet shadow.

The moon has words with the dogs.
She is mistaken and begins over.

Yesterday, tomorrow, black, and green
Troop around my circle of laurel.

Where would you look for my lifetime
If I exchanged my heart?

—And the figtree shouts at me and advances
Terrible and extended.

A Diamond

A Translation for Robert Jones

A diamond
Is there
At the heart of the moon or the branches or my nakedness
And there is nothing in the universe like diamond
Nothing in the whole mind.

The poem is a seagull resting on a pier at the end of the
ocean.

A dog howls at the moon
A dog howls at the branches
A dog howls at the nakedness
A dog howling with pure mind.

I ask for the poem to be as pure as a seagull's belly.

The universe falls apart and discloses a diamond
Two words called seagull are peacefully floating out where
the waves are.
The dog is dead there with the moon, with the branches,
with my nakedness
And there is nothing in the universe like diamond
Nothing in the whole mind.

The Little Halfwit

A Translation for Robin Blaser

I said, "Afternoon"
But it wasn't there.
The afternoon was another thing
Which had gone someplace.

(And the light shrugged its shoulders
Like a little girl.)

"Afternoon" But this is useless,
This is untrue, this has to it
Half a moon of lead. The other
Will never get here.

(And the light that everyone sees
Played at being a statue.)

The other one was tiny
And ate pomegranates.

This one is big and green and I'm not able
To grab her in my arms or dress her.
Is she ever coming? What was she?

(And the light as it went along, as a joke
Separated the little halfwit from his own shadow.)

Verlaine

A Translation for Pat Wilson

A song
Which I shall never sing
Has fallen asleep on my lips.
A song
Which I shall never sing—

Above the honeysuckle
There's a firefly
And the moon stings
With a ray into the water—

At that time I'll imagine
The song
Which I shall never sing.

A song full of lips
And far-off washes

A song full of lost
Hours in the shadow

A song of a star that's alive
Above enduring day.

Dear Lorca,

When I translate one of your poems and I come across words I do not understand, I always guess at their meanings. I am inevitably right. A really perfect poem (no one yet has written one) could be perfectly translated by a person who did not know one word of the language it was written in. A really perfect poem has an infinitely small vocabulary.

It is very difficult. We want to transfer the immediate object, the immediate emotion to the poem—and yet the immediate always has hundreds of its own words clinging to it, short-lived and tenacious as barnacles. And it is wrong to scrape them off and substitute others. A poet is a time mechanic not an embalmer. The words around the immediate shrivel and decay like flesh around the body. No mummy-sheet of tradition can be used to stop the process. Objects, words must be led across time not preserved against it.

I yell "Shit" down a cliff at an ocean. Even in my lifetime the immediacy of that word will fade. It will be dead as "Alas." But if I put the real cliff and the real ocean into the poem, the word "Shit" will ride along with them, travel the time-machine until cliffs and oceans disappear.

Most of my friends like words too well. They set them under the blinding light of the poem and try to extract every possible connotation from each of them, every temporary pun, every direct or indirect connection—as if a word could become an object by mere addition of consequences. Others pick up words from the street, from their bars, from their offices and display them proudly in their poems as if they were shouting, "See what I have collected from the American language. Look at my butterflies, my stamps, my old shoes!" What does one do with all this crap?

Words are what sticks to the real. We use them to push the real, to drag the real into the poem. They are what we hold on with, nothing else. They are as valuable in themselves as rope with nothing to be tied to.

I repeat—the perfect poem has an infinitely small vocabulary.

Love,
Jack

The Ballad of the Dead Woodcutter

A Translation for Louis Marbury

Because the figtree was sapless
It has cracked at the root.

Oh, you have fallen down on your head
You have fallen on your head.

Because the oaktree was rootless
It has cracked at the branch.

Oh, you have fallen down on your head
You have fallen on your head.

Because I walked through the branches
I have scratched out my heart.

Oh, you have fallen down on your head
You have fallen on your head.

The Ballad of Weeping

A Translation for Bob Connor

I have closed my window
Because I do not want to hear the weeping
But behind the gray walls
Nothing can be heard but weeping.

A few dogs might bark
A few angels might sing
There might be room for a thousand violins in the
    palm of my hand.

But the weeping is a big dog
The weeping is a big angel
The weeping is a big violin
The tears put a muzzle on the air
And nothing can be heard but weeping.

Alba

A Translation for Russ Fitzgerald

If your hand had been meaningless
Not a single blade of grass
Would spring from the earth's surface.
Easy to write, to kiss—
No, I said, read your paper.
Be there
Like the earth
When shadow covers the wet grass.

Song of the Poor

A Translation

Ay qué trabajo me cuesta
quererte como te quiero!

Because I love you the table
And the heart and the lamplight
Feel sorry for me.

Who will buy from me
That small belt I have
And that sadness of white thread
To weave handkerchiefs?

Because I love you the ceiling
And the heart and the air
Feel sorry for me.

Ay qué trabajo me cuesta
quererte como te quiero!

Ode for Walt Whitman

A Translation for Steve Jonas

Along East River and the Bronx
The kids were singing, showing off their bodies
At the wheel, at oil, the rawhide, and the hammer.
Ninety thousand miners were drawing silver out of boulders
While children made perspective drawings of stairways.

But no one went to sleep
No one wanted to be a river
No one loved the big leaves, no one
The blue tongue of the coastline.

Along East River into Queens
The kids were wrestling with industry.
The Jews sold circumcision's rose
To the faun of the river.
The sky flowed through the bridges and rooftops—
Herds of buffalo the wind was pushing.

But none of them would stay.
No one wanted to be cloud. No one
Looked for the ferns
Or the yellow wheel of the drum.

But if the moon comes out
The pulleys will slide around to disturb the sky
A limit of needles will fence in your memory
And there will be coffins to carry out your unemployed.

New York of mud,
New York of wire fences and death,
What angel do you carry hidden in your cheek?

What perfect voice will tell you the truth about wheat
Or the terrible sleep of your wet-dreamed anemones?

Not for one moment, beautiful old Walt Whitman,
Have I stopped seeing your beard full of butterflies
Or your shoulders of corduroy worn thin by the moon
Or your muscles of a virgin Apollo
Or your voice like a column of ashes
Ancient and beautiful as the fog.

You gave a cry like a bird
With his prick pierced through by a needle
Enemy of satyrs
Enemy of the grape
And lover of bodies under rough cloth.
Not for one moment, tight-cocked beauty,
Who in mountains of coal, advertisements, and railroads
Had dreamed of being a river and of sleeping like one
With a particular comrade, one who could put in your bosom
The young pain of an ignorant leopard.
Not for one moment, blood-Adam, male,
Man alone in the sea, beautiful
Old Walt Whitman.
Because on the rooftops
Bunched together in bars
Pouring out in clusters from toilets
Trembling between the legs of taxi-drivers
Or spinning upon platforms of whiskey
The cocksuckers, Walt Whitman, were counting on you.

That one also, also. And they throw themselves down on
Your burning virgin beard,
Blonds of the North, negroes from the seashore,
Crowds of shouts and gestures

Like cats or snakes
The cocksuckers, Walt Whitman, the cocksuckers,
Muddy with tears, meat for the whip,
Tooth or boot of the cowboys.

That one also, also. Painted fingers
Sprout out along the beach of your dreams
And you give a friend an apple
Which tastes faintly of gas-fumes
And the sun sings a song for the bellybuttons
Of the little boys who play games below bridges.

But you weren't looking for the scratched eyes
Or the blackswamp-country where children are sinking
Or the frozen spit
Or the wounded curves like a toad's paunch
Which cocksuckers wear in bars and night-clubs
While the moon beats them along the corners of terror.

You were looking for a naked man who would be like a river
Bull and dream, a connection between the wheel and the
    seaweed,
Be father for your agony, your death's camellia
And moan in the flames of your hidden equator.

For it is just that a man not look for his pleasure
In the forest of blood of the following morning.
The sky has coastlines where life can be avoided
And some bodies must not repeat themselves at sunrise.

Agony, agony, dream, leaven, and dream.
That is the world, my friend, agony, agony.
The dead decompose themselves under the clock of the
    cities.

War enters weeping, with a million gray rats.
The rich give to their girlfriends
Tiny illuminated dyings
And life is not noble, or good, or sacred.

A man is able if he wishes to lead his desire
Through vein of coral or the celestial naked.
Tomorrow his loves will be rock and Time
A breeze that comes sleeping through their clusters.

That is why I do not cry out, old Walt Whitman,
Against the little boy who writes
A girl's name on his pillow,
Or the kid who puts on a wedding dress
In the darkness of a closet
Or the lonely men in bars
Who drink with sickness the waters of prostitution
Or the men with green eyelids
Who love men and scald their lips in silence,
But against the rest of you, cocksuckers of cities,
Hard-up and dirty-brained,
Mothers of mud, harpies, dreamless enemies
Of the Love that distributes crowns of gladness.

Against the rest of you always, who give the kids
Drippings of sucked-off death with sour poison.
Against the rest of you always
Fairies of North America,
Pajaros of Havana,
Jotos of Mexico,
Sarasas of Cadiz,
Apios of Seville,
Cancos of Madrid,
Adelaidas of Portugal,

Cocksuckers of all the world, assassins of doves,
Slaves of women, lapdogs of their dressing tables,
Opening their flys in parks with a fever of fans
Or ambushed in the rigid landscapes of poison.

Let there be no mercy. Death
Trickles from all of your eyes, groups
Itself like gray flowers on beaches of mud.
Let there be no mercy. Watch out for them.
Let the bewildered, the pure,
The classical, the appointed, the praying
Lock the gates of this Bacchanalia.

And you, beautiful Walt Whitman, sleep on the banks of
    the Hudson
With your beard toward the pole and your palms open
Soft clay or snow, your tongue is invoking
Comrades to keep vigil over your gazelle without body.
Sleep, there is nothing left here.
A dance of walls shakes across the prairies
And America drowns itself with machines and weeping.
Let the hard air of midnight
Sweep away all the flowers and letters from the arch in
    which you sleep
And a little black boy announce to the white men of gold
The arrival of the reign of the ear of wheat.

Aquatic Park

A Translation for Jack Spicer

A green boat
Fishing in blue water

The gulls circle the pier
Calling their hunger

A wind rises from the west
Like the passing of desire

Two boys play on the beach
Laughing

Their gangling legs cast shadows
On the wet sand

Then,
Sprawling in the boat

A beautiful black fish.

Forest

A Translation for Joe Dunn

You want me to tell you
The secret of springtime—

And I relate to that secret
Like a high-branching firtree

Whose thousand little fingers
Point a thousand little roads.

I will tell you never, my love,
Because the river runs slowly

But I shall put into my branching voice
The ashy sky of your gaze.

Turn me around, brown child
Be careful of my needles.

Turn me around and around, playing
At the well pump of love.

The secret of springtime. How
I wish I could tell you!

Dear Lorca,

I would like to make poems out of real objects. The lemon to be a lemon that the reader could cut or squeeze or taste—a real lemon like a newspaper in a collage is a real newspaper. I would like the moon in my poems to be a real moon, one which could be suddenly covered with a cloud that has nothing to do with the poem—a moon utterly independent of images. The imagination pictures the real. I would like to point to the real, disclose it, to make a poem that has no sound in it but the pointing of a finger.

We have both tried to be independent of images (you from the start and I only when I grew old enough to tire of trying to make things connect), to make things visible rather than to make pictures of them (phantasia non imaginari). How easy it is in erotic musings or in the truer imagination of a dream to invent a beautiful boy. How difficult to take a boy in a blue bathing suit that I have watched as casually as a tree and to make him visible in a poem as a tree is visible, not as an image or a picture but as something alive—caught forever in the structure of words. Live moons, live lemons, live boys in bathing suits. The poem is a collage of the real.

But things decay, reason argues. Real things become garbage. The piece of lemon you shellac to the canvas begins to develop a mold, the newspaper tells of incredibly ancient events in forgotten slang, the boy becomes a grandfather. Yes, but the garbage of the real still reaches out into the current world making *its* objects, in turn, visible—lemon calls to lemon, newspaper to newspaper, boy to boy. As things decay they bring their equivalents into being.

Things do not connect; they correspond. That is what makes it possible for a poet to translate real objects, to bring them across language as easily as he can bring them across time. That tree you saw in Spain is a tree I could never have seen in California, that lemon has a different smell and a different taste, BUT the answer is this—every place and every time has a real object to *correspond* with your real object— that lemon may become this lemon, or it may even become this piece of seaweed, or this particular color of gray in this ocean. One does not need to imagine that lemon; one needs to discover it.

Even these letters. They *correspond* with something (I don't know what) that you have written (perhaps as unapparently as that lemon corresponds to this piece of seaweed) and, in turn, some future poet will write something which *corresponds* to them. That is how we dead men write to each other.

Love,
Jack

Narcissus

A Translation for Basil King

Poor Narcissus
Your dim fragrance
And the dim heart of the river

I want to stay at your edge
Flower of love
Poor Narcissus

Ripples and sleeping fish
Cross your white eyes
Songbirds and butterflies
Japanese mine

I so tall beside you
Flower of love
Poor Narcissus

How wide-awake the frogs are
They won't stay out of the surface
In which your madness and my madness
Mirrors itself

Poor Narcissus
My sorrow
Self of my sorrow.

He Died at Sunrise

A Translation for Allen Joyce

Night of four moons
And a single tree,
With a single shadow
And a single bird.

I look into my body for
The tracks of your lips.
A stream kisses into the wind
Without touch.

I carry the No you gave me
Clenched in my palm
Like something made of wax
An almost-white lemon.

Night of four moons
And a single tree
At the point of a needle
Is my love, spinning.

Ballad of the Terrible Presence

A Translation for Joe LeSueur

I want the river lost from its bed
I want the wind lost from its valleys

I want the night to be there without eyes
And my heart without the golden flower

So that the oxen talk with big leaves
And the earthworm is dead of shadow

So that the teeth of the skull glisten
And the yellows give a complete color to silk.

I can look at the agony of wounded night
Struggling, twisted up against noontime

I can stand all the sunsets of green poison
And the wornout rainbows that time suffers

But don't make your clean body too visible
Like a black cactus opened out among rushes

Let me go in an anguish of star clusters
Lose me. But don't show me that cool flesh.

Ballad of Sleeping Somewhere Else

A Translation for Ebbe Borregaard

The pine needles fall
Like an ax in the forest.

Can you hear them crumble
There where we are sleeping?

The windows are close to the wall
Here in the darkness they remain open.

(When I saw you in the morning
My arms were full of paper.)

Five hundred miles away
The moon is a hatchet of silver.

(When I saw you in the morning
My eyes were full of paper.)

Here the walls are firm
They do not crumble and remain certain.

(When I saw you in the morning
My heart was full of paper.)

Five hundred miles away
The stars are glass that is breaking.

The windows sag on the wall
I feel cold glass in the blankets.

Child, you are too tall for this bed.

The pine needles fall
Like an ax in the forest.

Can you hear them crumble
There where we are sleeping?

Dear Lorca,

When you had finished a poem what did it want you to do with it? Was it happy enough merely to exist or did it demand imperiously that you share it with somebody like the beauty of a beautiful person forces him to search the world for someone that can declare that beauty? And where did your poems find people?

Some poems are easily laid. They will give themselves to anybody and anybody physically capable can receive them. They may be beautiful (we have both written some that were) but they are meretricious. From the moment of their conception they inform us in a dulcet voice that, thank you, they can take care of themselves. I swear that if one of them were hidden beneath my carpet, it would shout out and seduce somebody. The quiet poems are what I worry about—the ones that must be seduced. They could travel about with me for years and no one would notice them. And yet, properly wed, they are more beautiful than their whorish cousins.

But I am speaking of the first night, when I leave my apartment almost breathless, searching for someone to show the poem to. Often now there is no one. My fellow poets (those I showed poetry to ten years ago) are as little interested in my poetry as I am in theirs. We both compare the poems shown (unfavorably, of course) with the poems we were writing ten years ago when we could learn from each other. We are polite but it is as if we were trading snapshots of our children—old acquaintances who disapprove of each other's wives. Or were you more generous, García Lorca?

There are the young, of course. I have been reduced to them (or my poems have) lately. The advantage in them is that they haven't yet decided what kind of poetry they are going to write tomorrow and are always looking for some device of yours to use. Yours, that's the trouble. Yours and not the poem's. They read the poem once to catch the marks of your style and then again, if they are at all pretty, to see if there is any reference to them in the poem. That's all. I know. I used to do it myself.

When you are in love there is no real problem. The person you love is always interested because he knows that the poems are always about him. If only because each poem will someday be said to belong to the Miss X or Mr. Y period of the poet's life. I may not be a better poet when I am in love, but I am a far less frustrated one. My poems have an audience.

Finally there are friends. There have only been two of them in my life who could read my poems and one of that two really prefers to put them in print so he can see them better. The other is far away.

All this is to explain why I dedicate each of our poems to someone.

Love,
Jack

Narcissus

A Translation for Richard Rummonds

Child,
How you keep falling into rivers.

At the bottom there's a rose
And in the rose there's another river.

Look at that bird. Look,
That yellow bird.

My eyes have fallen down
Into the water.

My god,
How they're slipping! Youngster!

—And I'm in the rose myself.

When I was lost in water I
Understood but won't tell you.

Ballad of the Dead Boy

A Translation for Graham Mackintosh

Every afternoon in Granada
Every afternoon a boy dies
Every afternoon the river sits itself down
To talk things over with its neighbors.

All the dead wear wings of moss.
The cloudy wind and the bright wind
Are two pheasants who fly around towers
And the day is a boy with a wound in him.

There wasn't a touch of lark in the sky
When I met you at the wine cavern
Or a fragment of cloud near the earth
When you drowned on the river.

A giant of water went slopping over the mountains
And the canyon spun around the dogs and lilies.
Your body, with the violet shadow of my hands,
Was dead there on the banks, an archangel, cold.

Song for September

A Translation for Don Allen

In the distant night the children are singing:
    A little river
    And a colored fountain

THE CHILDREN: When will our hearts come back from
    your holiday?

I: When my words no longer need me.

THE CHILDREN: You have left us here to sing the death of
    your summer
    A little river
    And a colored fountain
        What September flowers do you hold in your hand?

I: A bloody rose and a white lily.

THE CHILDREN: Dip them in the water of an old song
    A little river
    And a colored fountain
        What are you tasting in your thirsty mouth?

I: The flavor of the bones of my big skull.

THE CHILDREN: Drink the kind water of an old song
    A little river
    And a colored fountain
        Why have you gone so very far from the death of
        your summer?

I: I am looking for a magical clockworkman.

THE CHILDREN: And how will you find the highway of
  poets?

I: The fountain and a river and an old song.

THE CHILDREN: You are going very far.

I: I am going very far, farther than my poems, farther than
  the mountains, farther than the birds. I am going to ask
  Christ to give me back my childhood, ripe with
  sunburn and feathers and a wooden sword.

THE CHILDREN: You have left us here to sing the death of
  your summer. And you will never return.
  A little river
  And a colored fountain
      And you will never return.

Buster Keaton Rides Again: A Sequel

A Translation for The Big Cat Up There

BUSTER KEATON (entering a long dark corridor): This must be Room 73.

PIGEON: Sir, I am a pigeon.

BUSTER KEATON (taking a dictionary out of his back pocket): I don't understand what anybody is talking about.

(No one rides by on a bicycle. The corridor is quite silent.)

PIGEON: I have to go to the bathroom.

BUSTER KEATON: In a minute.

(Two chambermaids come by carrying towels. They give one to the pigeon and one to Buster Keaton.)

1ST CHAMBERMAID: Why do you suppose human beings have lips?

2ND CHAMBERMAID: Nothing like that entered my head.

BUSTER KEATON: No. There were supposed to be three chambermaids.

(He takes out a chessboard and begins playing upon it.)

PIGEON: I could love you if I were a dove.

BUSTER KEATON (biting the chessboard): When I was a child I was put in jail for not giving information to the police.

3 CHAMBERMAIDS: Yes.

BUSTER KEATON: I am not a Catholic.

PIGEON: Don't you believe that God died?

BUSTER KEATON (crying): No.

(4 Spanish dancers come in. They are mostly male.)

1ST SPANISH DANCER: I have a little magazine up my ass.

4 CHAMBERMAIDS: Oh!

(Buster Keaton forgets his politeness and becomes a Catholic. He takes mass, says Holy Mary Mother of God, and distributes rosaries to all the policemen in the room. He hangs by his heels from a crucifix.)

VIRGIN MARY (coming in abruptly): Buster Keaton you have $_bu^mp_ed$ The Car.

BUSTER KEATON: No.

(Alcohol comes in wearing the disguise of a cockroach. It is blue. It crawls silently up Buster Keaton's leg.)

BUSTER KEATON: No.

(Alcohol and the Virgin Mary perform a dance. They both pretend to have been lovers.)

BUSTER KEATON: I will never see either of you in Rockland. I am not going to Rockland.

(He takes the chessboard and invents a new alphabet.)

VIRGIN MARY: Holy Mary Mother of God Pray For Us Sinners Now At The Hour Of Our Death.

ALCOHOL: Dada is as dada does.

VIRGIN MARY: Did. (She falls into a blue robe.)

BUSTER KEATON: I wonder if there is anything but love in the universe.

(Suddenly, at the last possible time before the curtain falls, somebody kisses the Virgin Mary, and Buster Keaton, and everybody.)

ALCOHOL: If I weren't tone-deaf I would sing.

BUSTER KEATON (sadly): I announce a new world.

(Three literary critics disguised as chambermaids bring down the curtain. Buster Keaton, bleeding, breaks through the curtain. He stands in the middle of the stage holding a fresh pomegranate in his arms.)

BUSTER KEATON (even more sadly): I announce the death of Orpheus.

(Everyone comes in. Policemen, waitresses, and Irene Tavener. They perform a complicated symbolic dance. Alcohol nibbles at the legs of every dancer.)

BUSTER KEATON (bleeding profusely): I love you. I love you. (As a last effort he throws the bleeding pomegranate from his heart.) No kidding, I love you.

VIRGIN MARY (taking him into her arms): You have b^u^mp^e_d the car.

(The gaudy blue curtain, silent and alive like the mouth of a seagull, covers everything.)

The Ballad of Escape

A Translation for Nat Harden

I have become lost many times along the ocean
With my ears filled with newly cut flowers
With my tongue full of loving and agony
I have become lost many times along the ocean
Like I lose myself in the hearts of some boys.

There is no night in which, giving a kiss,
One does not feel the smiles of the faceless people
And there is no one in touching something recently born
Who can quite forget the motionless skulls of horses.

Because the roses always search in the forehead
For a hard landscape of bone
And the hands of a man have no other purpose
Than to be like the roots that grow beneath wheat-fields.

Like I lose myself in the hearts of some boys
I have become lost many times along the ocean
Along the vastness of water I wander searching
An end to the lives that have tried to complete me.

Venus

A Translation for Ann Simon

The dead girl
In the winding shell of the bed
Naked of the little wind and flowers
Surges on into perennial light.

The world stayed behind
Lily of cotton and shadow.
It peeked timidly out of the mirror
Looking on at that infinite passage.

The dead girl
Was eaten from inside by love.
In the unyieldingness of seafoam
She lost her hair.

Friday, the 13th

A Translation for Will Holther

At the base of the throat is a little machine
Which makes us able to say anything.
Below it are carpets
Red, blue, and green-colored.
I say the flesh is not grass.
It is an empty house
In which there is nothing
But a little machine
And big, dark carpets.

Song of Two Windows

A Translation for James Broughton

Wind, window, moon
(I open the window to the sky)
Wind, window, moon
(I open the window to the earth)
Then
From the sky
The voices of two girls.

In the middle of my mirror
A girl is drowning
The voice of a single girl.
She holds cold fire like a glass
Each thing she watches
Has become double.
Cold fire is
Cold fire is.
In the middle of my mirror
A girl is drowning
The voice of a single girl.

A branch of night
Enters through my window
A great dark branch
With bracelets of water
Behind a blue mirror
Someone is drowning
The wounded instants
Along the clock—pass.

I stick my head out of the window and I see a chopper of wind ready to cut it off. Upon that invisible guillotine I have mounted the heads without eyes of all my desires, and the odor of lemon fills all of the instant while the wind changes to a flower of gas.

At the pool there has died
A girl of water
She has pushed the earth aside
Like a ripe apple
Down from her head to her thighs
A fish crosses her, calling softly
The wind whispers, "Darling"
But is unable to awaken her

The pool holds loosely
Its rider of something
And in the air its gray nipples
Vibrate with frogs.
God, we hail you. We will make payment
To Our Lady of Water
For the girl in the pool
Dead below the ripples.
I will soon put at her side
Two small gourds
Because they can keep afloat,
Yes, even in water.

Dear Lorca,

Loneliness is necessary for pure poetry. When someone intrudes into the poet's life (and any sudden personal contact, whether in the bed or in the heart, is an intrusion) he loses his balance for a moment, slips into being who he is, uses his poetry as one would use money or sympathy. The person who writes the poetry emerges, tentatively, like a hermit crab from a conch shell. The poet, for that instant, ceases to be a dead man.

I, for example, could not finish the last letter I was writing you about sounds. You were like a friend in a distant city to whom I was suddenly unable to write, not because the fabric of my life had changed, but because I was suddenly, temporarily, not in the fabric of my life. I could not tell you about it because both it and I were momentary.

Even the objects change. The seagulls, the greenness of the ocean, the fish—they become things to be traded for a smile or the sound of conversation—counters rather than objects. Nothing matters except the big lie of the personal—the lie in which these objects do not believe.

That instant, I said. It may last for a minute, a night, or a month, but, this I promise you, García Lorca, the loneliness returns. The poet encysts the intruder. The objects come back to their own places, silent and unsmiling. I again begin to write you a letter on the sound of a poem. And this immediate thing, this personal adventure, will not have been transferred into the poem like the waves and the birds were, will, at best, show in the lovely pattern of cracks in some poem where autobiography shattered but did not quite destroy the surface. And the encysted emotion will itself become an object, to be transferred at last into poetry like the waves and the birds.

And I will again become your special comrade.

Love,
Jack

The Moon and Lady Death

A Translation for Helen Adam

The moon has marble teeth
How old and sad she looks!
There is a dry river
There is a hill without grass
There is a dead oak tree
Near a dry river.

Lady Death, wrinkled,
Goes looking for custom
At the heels of a crowd
Of tenuous phantoms.
Near the dead oak tree
Near the dry river
There is a fair without trumpets
And tents made of shadow.

She sells them dry paint
Made of wax and torture,
Wicked and twisted
Like a witch in a story.
There is a dry river
There is a hill without grass
There is a dead oak tree
Near a dry river.

The moon
Is tossing money
Down through the black air.
Near the dead oak tree
Near the dry river

There is a fair without trumpets
And tents made of shadow.

Afternoon

A Translation for John Barrow

The sky asks afternoon for a word.
—"It is 1:36. A black cloud
Has crossed one of the white clouds.
13 empty boats
And a seagull."

The bay asks afternoon for a word.
—"The wind is blowing
Southwest at nine miles an hour
I am in love with an ocean
Whose heart is the color of wet sand.
At 1:37
13 empty boats
And a seagull."

Afternoon asks the ocean,
"Why does a man die?"
—"It is 1:37
13 empty boats
And a seagull."

Dear Lorca,

This is the last letter. The connection between us, which had been fading away with the summer, is now finally broken. I turn in anger and dissatisfaction to the things of my life and you return, a disembodied but contagious spirit, to the printed page. It is over, this intimate communion with the ghost of García Lorca, and I wonder now how it was ever able to happen.

It was a game, I shout to myself. A game. There are no angels, ghosts, or even shadows. It was a game made out of summer and freedom and a need for a poetry that would be more than the expression of my hatreds and desires. It was a game like Yeats' spooks or Blake's sexless seraphim.

Yet it was there. The poems are there, the memory not of a vision but a kind of casual friendship with an undramatic ghost who occasionally looked through my eyes and whispered to me, not really more important then than my other friends, but now achieving a different level of reality by being missing. Today, alone by myself, it is like having lost a pair of eyes and a lover.

What is real, I suppose, will endure. Poe's mechanical chessplayer was not the less a miracle for having a man inside it, and when the man departed, the games it had played were no less beautiful. The analogy is false, of course, but it holds both a promise and a warning for each of us.

It is October now. Summer is over. Almost every trace of the months that produced these poems has been obliterated. Only explanations are possible, only regrets.

Saying goodbye to a ghost is more final than saying goodbye to a lover. Even the dead return, but a ghost, once loved, departing will never reappear.

Love,
Jack

Radar

A Postscript for Marianne Moore

No one exactly knows
Exactly how clouds look in the sky
Or the shape of the mountains below them
Or the direction in which fish swim.
No one exactly knows.
The eye is jealous of whatever moves
And the heart
Is too far buried in the sand
To tell.

They are going on a journey
Those deep blue creatures
Passing us as if they were sunshine
Look
Those fins, those closed eyes
Admiring each last drop of the ocean.

I crawled into bed with sorrow that night
Couldn't touch his fingers. See the splash
Of the water
The noisy movement of cloud
The push of the humpbacked mountains
Deep at the sand's edge.

DANTE ALIGHIERI THE NEW LIFE
Translated by Dante Gabriel Rossetti; Preface by Michael Palmer

KINGSLEY AMIS COLLECTED POEMS: 1944–1979

GUILLAUME APOLLINAIRE ZONE: SELECTED POEMS
Translated by Ron Padgett

AUSTERITY MEASURES THE NEW GREEK POETRY
Edited by Karen Van Dyck

SZILÁRD BORBÉLY BERLIN-HAMLET
Translated by Ottilie Mulzet

MARGARET CAVENDISH *Edited by Michael Robbins*

NAJWAN DARWISH NOTHING MORE TO LOSE
Translated by Kareem James Abu-Zeid

NAJWAN DARWISH EXHAUSTED ON THE CROSS
Translated by Kareem James Abu-Zeid; Foreword by Raúl Zurita

BENJAMIN FONDANE CINEPOEMS AND OTHERS
Edited by Leonard Schwartz

PERE GIMFERRER *Translated by Adrian Nathan West*

W. S. GRAHAM *Selected by Michael Hofmann*

SAKUTARŌ HAGIWARA CAT TOWN
Translated by Hiroaki Sato

MICHAEL HELLER TELESCOPE: SELECTED POEMS

MIGUEL HERNÁNDEZ *Selected and translated by Don Share*

RICHARD HOWARD RH ♥ HJ AND OTHER AMERICAN WRITERS
Introduction by Timothy Donnelly